Live Life For a Living

An inspirational guide
to help turn dreams into reality
by Lynnette Rozine Prock

Dedicated to my husband, Ayman
and my best friend, Bunny Love.

To those who dare to dream
with an open heart and open mind.

In honor of my Great Aunt Marie

In memory of my biggest inspiration,
my Mom

Thank you to my editors:
Emily Bennett and Michelle Chevallier

Published by Lynnette Rozine Prock
Los Angeles, California

i

ii

ISBN 9781470075262

6

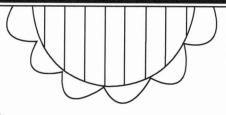

introduction

A lot of the suggestions and ideas in this book come from the perspective of an artist (who's turned her hobby into a career). Don't worry if you're not an artist type – you can also benefit from this book. If you have leadership qualities but are not recognized in the corporate world, there is insight for you here. If your goal is to lose ten pounds, but you don't know how you'll ever be able to do it, you can make discoveries from my advice. *Live Life For A Living* is about listening to your ideas, and trusting your thoughts and instincts. It's about having and building confidence in yourself, and acting on your instincts without fear. It's about doing what makes you happy, not what pleases others. This book will help you believe in yourself and know yourself. You will learn to recognize and enhance your strengths. You will pay attention to and overcome your weaknesses. Most importantly, you will be encouraged to enjoy your life. I believe your life is for you – not for your children, your parents, your spouse, your siblings or your boss. While all of these people may benefit from your existence, your life exists for *you*.

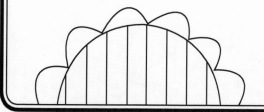

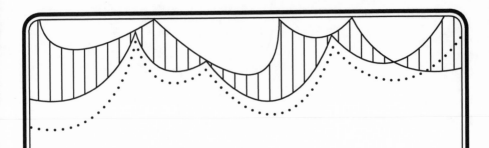

ROUTİNE

Do you remember when you were a kid, and anything and everything was possible? Remember how your imagination allowed you to believe that your empty backyard was a house, a war zone, or a fantasy forest? Remember how many things a simple box could be? Remember pillow forts; forts made out of cushions and blankets? Children are able to play and pretend, and escape the trap of time because they are not yet conditioned to routine schedules. Even if parents keep kids on a tight schedule, there are times when children rebel and resist. I have to assume that every child at one point in their lives complains about it being bedtime "already". We are not born with time being a governing law. We are not born with an inner voice that says, "It's Monday morning, you must begin your week." We are gradually conditioned to Monday morning. Time is taught to us.

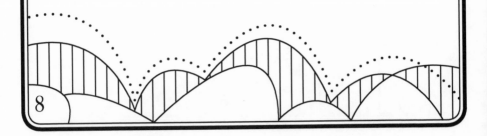

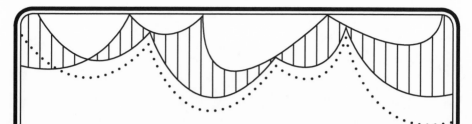

As children, we were free and flowing. We were not aware of minutes or hours, and in fact, whenever adults told us to wait just 15 minutes, we became confused. We had no instinctual feeling of what 15 minutes represented. How long is that, exactly? Sometimes 15 minutes felt like forever, while at other times, 15 minutes passed by quickly. As children, we cared about the current moment. We were focused on the exact moment that was happening to us right then and there, and future and past moments were unfamiliar to us. Remember how freeing and joyful that was? Why have we lost that? Where is that freedom, and when did we lose contact with the present moment?

As we grow older, society teaches us about time (mostly indirectly) but conditioning us in a way that tricks our minds into thinking routine is normal and usual. We go to school at a certain time, and each class or period is so many minutes long. We have lunch and recess at the same time, and we go home at exactly the same time every day. We have extra curricular activities on the same days of the week, and things become habitual. We have weekends free.

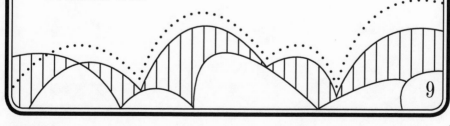

What this routine lifestyle does is train us to look forward to the weekend. "Thank God It's Friday", right? We can't wait for Saturday to come along, so we can break up the monotony of the routine! We can sleep in as long as we want. We can watch cartoons or go outside to play. We can finally garden, or work on our hobbies! We can catch up on our lives! We have a temporary freedom that we all look forward to for the entire stretch of the week. Our routines make the weekend this magical time. Saturday and Sunday become days we can go to the beach, or a day we can catch up on chores. We can go camping on the weekend, or we can relax and do nothing. We can throw parties, and celebrate events that happened during the week while we were too busy managing our routine.

Why is it that Monday mornings have such a bad reputation? Why are so many people resisting the beginning of the work week? Why is it that on Sunday nights, we dread waking up early to go to work in the morning? We all wish for a longer weekend and more time to catch up; more time to enjoy our lives. What is Monday, anyway? I mean, I can see it on a calendar. I know it's every seventh day. I know that a large percentage of businesses start their week on Monday. However, I don't think that it was created for these reasons. Wait — it *was* created. It didn't always exist!

So, when and why did we all decide to agree with society and say this is an okay way to live? Why can't every day be Saturday? Even in our adult lives, we look forward to holidays that give us an extra day off, so that we can have a three or four day weekend. We then go back to our routines and accept it as a way of life. People say, "Man, I wish that we worked three days a week and had four days off every week." But then, no one does anything about it. It is rare that anyone takes the action to make that "dream" their way of life!

Let's look deeper at that. "A way of life." That implies a choice, doesn't it? The saying is not "a 'force' of life" or "a 'law' of life". No, it's a way of life. There are many ways of life. The way of life for some people is a corporate life. Others prefer to be tattoo artists. Some are outdoorsy types, and others like monster trucks. There are choices we've made throughout our lives that define who we are. It's our way of life. Why then, are we allowing society the chance at determining our way of life? Why do we accept that a 40 hour, Monday-through-Friday routine is okay if we are internally rebelling against it?

I want to encourage you to seriously ponder this thought. I want you to succeed at recognizing that you *do* have a choice. You can make your life happen the way you want it to. You can have three days of work and four days off, if that is what you want.

Time is very convenient for many things, especially when other people are involved. You can't ask children to gather for math class "when they feel like it," and expect all of the students to show up at the same time. There is a time and a place for time. When you can escape the confines of time, you should. When you are free from obligation to large groups of people, you should set yourself free from schedules.

Bosses and managers depend on time, because it requires that all subordinates are at their desks when it is convenient for the job. Teachers need their students to be at the right place and at the right time. Of course, there are jobs where time is, in fact, necessary for efficiency. Factory work needs to be coordinated with the right amount of people in the right place, at the right time. Service jobs like waitressing, transportation and retail also require people to stick to a schedule. However, I don't know very many dreamers that think, "I can't *wait* to waitress for the rest of my life!"

We've all had a boss or manager that somehow seemed to completely take over our lives. If you are young, you can probably relate to this situation like that of having a parent that is pressuring you to get things done the way they want it. No matter what the situation, when under pressure from someone else's obligation, we are really thinking, "Just leave me alone and let me do what I want." Why not say this out loud? If doing what you love is really what you want to do, why aren't you? Really ask yourself this question.

Routines can easily become distractions from your dreams. They can be a coping mechanism that allows you to tell your dreams, "Hey, Dreams-That-Seem-Hard-To-Reach! I can't pay attention to you because I'm busy working 40 hours a week; going grocery shopping and commuting back and forth between work and my kid's extracurricular activities." What would happen if you told your structured schedules "Hey, Distraction-And-Meaningless-Use-Of-Energy (a.k.a. Routine)! I have dreams of creativity, happiness and joy. I'm going to do big things for myself and it's going to help the world be a better place!"? Let's get you to a place where you recognize how important this second statement is.

Even nature rebels against routine! Sure, we have four seasons, and every year certain months are colder than other months. Though there are yearly occurrences, they are never precise. There isn't a schedule where nature says, "Well, it's November 21st at 4:30pm. I have to turn down my thermostat and give a dusting of snow to parts of Chicago." Nature does not do this. Nature reacts to the environment accordingly. Flowers sprout from the ground when the weather is right. The skies drop snow when the weather is cold, and rain when the weather is warmer. The shape and size of clouds form based upon elements of the environment. There is pattern, and there is structure. There is discipline, but things happen in nature based on moments in the surrounding environment. Do you think that nature cares that it's the year 2000, 2020, or 1295 BC? I'm merely suggesting that there's an even greater acknowledgment and recognition for our human instincts.

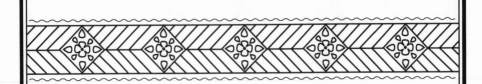

A lot of professionals claim that routines give children a sense of security and help keep children "calm". I can see that point. I understand the concept. However, I also know that growing up with non-conformist ideals and free-spirited behaviors was very comfortable and natural to me. One big struggle for me as a child was trying to understand those around me that were fighting time and organizing their every minute! It seemed so controlling and conflicting to me, as if those with rigid schedules were never *truly* enjoying themselves – even if the activities they were doing were their passions and hobbies.

In this day and age, parents hand children over to others to accommodate the adult routine lifestyle, which is very demanding in most cases. It is much easier and more convenient to numb a child's instinct by throwing them into a routine, rather than accommodating a child's random instinctual desires.

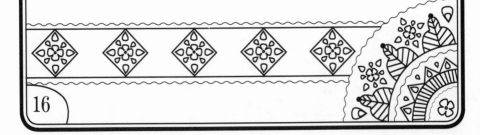

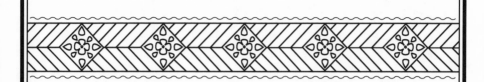

It is unrealistic to expect a parent (or family) to accommodate every whim of a child. It is much easier to set a routine and follow it. Even though sometimes it feel like juggling chainsaws – soccer today, gymnastics tomorrow, a birthday party on Friday, etc. – for the most part it allows a sense of freedom to a family, because it determines things far in advance. Nothing is left to chance or randomness. Everything becomes fated and scheduled. Routine eventually provides a chance to relax, because you can now schedule a vacation or a weekend getaway or nap! Routine defines our lives so that we don't have to think beyond "what's for dinner?" and "what time does Susie need to be picked up?"

One of the greatest lessons my mom taught me was that time is irrelevant. Time on a clock or from a calendar is man-made, and while schedules are appropriate for certain occasions, they should not dictate or confine our lives, or determine "what's next". We had a tremendous amount of freedom and flexibility growing up.

İNSTİNCTS

I want to inspire you to become closer to nature and your natural self. I want to help you remove old beliefs about society. I will encourage you to use time to your advantage, instead of as a disadvantage. I can help you use time wisely instead of feeling anxious about time (or lack of time).

Personally, I grew up in a home that functioned without clocks. Our mom did have one clock on the coffee pot, but that was not for her or for us. The clock told the coffee pot when it should brew coffee, so that when my mom woke up, the coffee would be ready for her. The clock was for the coffee. My mother had a digital alarm clock in her bedroom, but she always woke up before the alarm went off. We were raised to listen to and respond to our internal, biological clocks. In other words, we paid attention to our instincts. When we were tired, we went to bed. When we woke up, we got out of bed. When we were hungry, we went to the kitchen. When we were bored, we did something creative. When we felt lazy, we watched TV, and when we felt inspired, we did something productive. If we were full of energy, we did something active. We reacted to our internal gut feelings, thoughts and ideas.

I want you to start doing this. I want you to start reacting to your internal gut feelings, your thoughts and your ideas. I want you to become so aware of your own energy that you never need look at a clock or a calendar to determine what's going to happen next. I want you to pay attention to your body — your mind, your soul and your heart. Listen to the signals and then answer them.

Don't intimidate yourself by focusing on that final destination of peace, harmony and enlightenment. Take baby steps. For example: if you're sitting at the computer for too long and your eyes are starting to strain, get up and walk away. Look at something else. Take a break. Whatever you were doing on the computer will be there when you get back. Notice that your eyes are sending you a message that they are tired. If your house is chaotic from screaming children, loud television, or cranky family members, and you develop a headache from stress, get away from it all for an hour. Take a bath. Go for a walk.

Whatever you do, don't ignore these prompts from your body telling you to make a change in environment. Your body will tell you everything you need in order to find peace. Stop ignoring the signals! They are the key to your true happiness. They are the answer you've always searched for. They are your instincts and they will always tell you exactly what you need. Isn't that crazy? The answer has always been within you! You have been telling yourself what you need to be happy your whole life. But were you listening? It takes practice, but I know you can do it.

A television will tell you what you need. So will a magazine, a newspaper, the internet, your mother-in-law, your spouse, friends and neighbors. Everyone has an opinion. When you get a strange e-mail from an address you don't recognize, with a weird link attached, you don't bite. Why? Because you're smarter than that. You know what is best for you. You know a scam when you see it.

You also know when you love something – a food, a scent, a color, an activity, a song. You know *you*. So, listen to yourself! Go ahead and listen to all the other opinions, too. Take them in for what they are – other people's opinions – and ultimately, do what you know is best for you. Trust yourself. People all over the world will tell you what they think is best for you. They might even be right sometimes. But it's *your* life. You wake up with yourself every day. You go to sleep with yourself every night. Even if you think your partner or best friend knows you completely, they don't know you as well as you know yourself.

Another conscious behavioral change you can make which will help you get to living your dreams, is to start really paying attention to what is going on around you. Notice what is happening all around you. Really start to *listen* to the sound of wind rustling through trees. Hear the birds chirping and the squirrels scampering around. Look at the leaves on trees, and notice how they weren't so green last week. Don't wait until the obvious color change in the fall. Look at the trees every day. Start to look at all the details that you pass on your daily commute. How many stop signs do you go through? How many people are carpooling, versus those that drive alone in a car? When you eat, really notice how things taste. If you eat an apple every day, ask yourself if there is any difference in the taste or texture of the apple from one day to the next. Really start to quiz yourself about the details of things that are happening around you. What does the fabric on your chair feel like when you touch it? At what point in the day do your eyes start to get tired from staring at a computer? How long does it take before your feet start to notice that you've been standing for along time?

Once you start to slow down and notice sounds, sights and feelings, you'll begin to listen and communicate better. In the fast paced lifestyle of taking every sound for granted, it's common to draw a conclusion about a conversation before it's even finished. Once you are in the moment, you'll learn to fully listen to what another person is saying while they are saying it. You'll take the time to gather your thoughts and construct a graceful, smart and relevant response.

Your mind will begin to work more efficiently. You will be able to plan and schedule things. Wait — what's that you say? Isn't this book about anti-planning and anti-scheduling? Yes and no. I encourage you to break free from the trap of complying to other people's demands. I want you to make your own plans. Create your own schedules and do the things you desire. If you are able to break free from other people's demands but you aren't in tune with your own surroundings and instincts, you might notice that you don't know which direction to go. Your mind will be all over the place, and you will be unsure of what steps you need to take to get to your dream life.

Let's talk about an animal's life. Do animals wake up at 6:00 am because they have to be somewhere by 8:00? Do they think, "Oh, it's 10:00 pm. That's my bedtime! I had better go to sleep." That is silly and absurd. Unlike humans, time is irrelevant to animals! They eat when they have food in front of them, go to sleep when they are tired, and birds fly south when it gets cold. They are in touch with their biological clock and they listen to their instincts. Yes, humans are more evolved than animals and yes, time has its benefits, but my suggestion is to break the chains of enslavement to time and schedules. Use time to your advantage. Don't let time use you. Stop letting routines and schedules distract you from your true purpose. Reverse the habit — instead of checking your watch first, listen to your instincts first.

The same philosophy can be applied to holidays. Why give gifts only on birthdays, anniversaries and Christmas? Shouldn't we give gifts to someone we love when the opportunity is there? Does it make sense that when we see something that we know our coworker or family member would love, we buy it and then hold on to it until an appropriate holiday arrives? Shouldn't we just stay in the moment and react to what is in our immediate environment?

This concept is foreign to many people. A lot of people receive comfort from their schedules. A schedule keeps a person busy and organized. A schedule, in a way, gives people a purpose. Imagine if you cleared everything off your calendar. Would you feel free, or would you feel fear and anxiety, like you've lost your identity and purpose? Learn to keep appointments for organizational purposes. Release yourself from the obligation of doing things that are not in alignment with your dream life.

Tune into your biological clock. Listen to your inner self. When it's time to create, create. When it's time to get up and exercise, do just that. If you find comfort in a scheduled lifestyle, create a scheduled lifestyle for yourself. Base it on *your* needs – not your boss's needs, not your children's needs, or your parent's needs. Do what makes you happy.

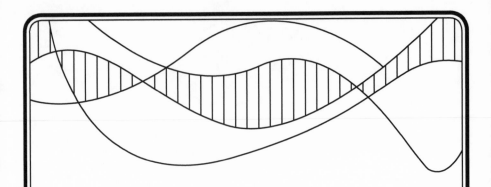

Please note that I am not promoting anarchy, total selfishness or disregard for others. The idea here is to stop doing what others expect of you, and to get back in touch with *your* true being and *your* true meaning. Create your life for you. Do not settle for complacency. Be nice to people, but don't make decisions based on what makes other people happy. The people around you will benefit from your personal growth and development. However, they may be trying to control you, in which case, they are not the kind of people you want to be around. We'll talk about that more later.

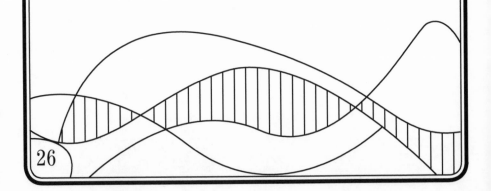

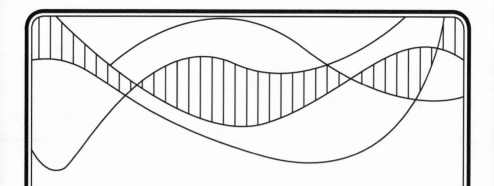

What does all of this have to do with making your dreams a reality anyway? Present-minded focus strengthens your instincts. When you schedule things to happen based on a routine, rather than reacting to moments as they happen, you ignore the instincts that are trying to encourage you to live your life fully and completely. Once you start paying attention to the things around you and the things inside you, you'll start to fully be able to recognize your dream's worth. You'll be able to take the actions that benefit that dream. You will see signs that may not make sense, but you'll recognize that these signs will lead you towards your goal, and you'll be able to consciously act on these instinctual notions.

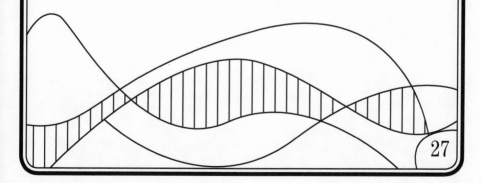

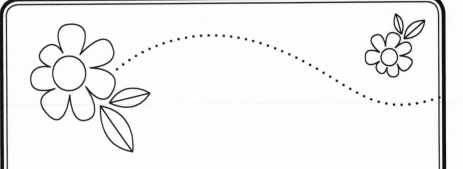

You will meet resistance. You will find yourself in situations that require you to rebel against society. You may do things that in past circumstances you would not have even considered. In your life before the realization that your dreams matter, you might have avoided conflict with your peers and/or superiors. Don't beat yourself up if this still happens. Instead, pay attention to it. Notice your resistance. After a while, you will grow stronger and more confident about what *you* know is right for you, versus what other people are telling you is right for you. You may need to get up and walk around the office once every hour to rest your eyes, neck and brain. You might even start to take more time off from work. You may need to tell your family to "chill" for a bit while you clear your mind. Trust me; they'll get over it — and you'll be better for it.

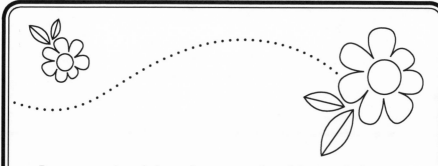

I am not implying that you should wreak havoc, destroy relationships or ruin your career. I don't encourage anyone to take dramatic actions or make gigantic changes quickly. I am simply asking you to increase your awareness, little by little, about what society dictates versus what your instinctual impulses ask you to do. Soon you will be questioning everything. You'll notice that you see, hear, feel, taste and smell things that were disguised before. All of a sudden, you'll notice your body has signals. Your senses will become heightened. You'll see new beauties. You'll feel from a far deeper place than ever before. Your mind, body and soul will thank you for paying attention, and you will be rewarded. All of these things that you'll see, feel, smell and hear have existed before. They were always around you. But you were numb. Once you retrain and awaken your instincts, you'll see so much joy and beauty that you won't ever go back to being a zombie.

If humans always agreed with what society dictates, we'd still think the world was flat. Europeans would never have left to discover new lands. Slaves would not be free. Women would not be able to vote. Modern technology would not even be available if humans remained content. The people that start revolutions and rebellions trust their instincts. They believe that society's standards are not acceptable. They want a better world to live in. They act on those instincts, and let it be known to the world that how they feel inside is truer than what society is imposing on them.

I remember my favorite story about getting a job, which was not through the usual routes of looking online or in newspapers at the classified ads. Instead I had asked myself, "What do you want to do?" I drove past a stained glass studio and said to myself, "I want to do *that*!" What did I do? I looked in the Yellow Pages of the phone book, called every single stained glass artist in the greater Chicago area, and asked if they needed help. Most of my phone calls ended with rejection, and left me feeling frustrated and doubting my choices. Could I really just call places that I wanted to work at and expect to get a job? Well, apparently I could. One phone call answered with a "yes." In fact, they were looking for help in their show room, and asked if I could possibly come down to meet them. It turns out they were desperately looking for someone *just like me* to come work in their showroom. The job was not for an artist, but instead was for a sales rep to work in the showroom. The artists were back in the studio creating stained glass wonders. It wasn't exactly what I had in mind when I decided that I wanted to work at a stained glass studio, but I was proud of myself for doing something unconventionally. I wanted something. I went for it. I got it!

I went to work and waited for customers to come in. They rarely came in. I found myself in a showroom full of colored glass, cutters, sanders and grout. Since I don't allow myself to become bored, I started experimenting with the tools and some scrap pieces of glass. My tinkering was noticed by the owner of the shop, and he expanded my tools and supplies to include anything in the shop that I wanted to use. I started making mirrors framed with glass mosaics. I made an "OPEN" sign for the shop, and even designed two door panels for a margarita bar. My determination to do what made me happy (versus what society expected of me) lead to pieces of stained glass art that I designed being hung in a very hip and trendy bar in Chicago! My will to do what I wanted to do with my life led me to having things I wanted to have in my life. It seems so simple!

Where would I be now, had I thought, "I want to work at a stained glass factory" and then followed that with, "Yeah, but how?" or "I don't have any experience doing that," or "The economy is bad; no one's hiring." I could have easily given up after a few phone calls that ended in rejection. Where would I be if I had made excuses or listened to any fear or doubt? I certainly wouldn't be here writing this story.

DREAMS

First and foremost, we need to figure out what you want to do. Try to remember that dream you had as a child. Imagine a goal you always wanted to accomplish. If you're not already doing it, we can assume that somewhere along the line, society (friends, family, or colleagues) discouraged you from pursuing this dream. Perhaps your likes and dislikes changed. You may have given in to fear. Whatever the case; find what makes you insanely happy and gives you the most joy. Do not allow discouragement into your thinking. Your influenced brain might remind you about rent, or the cost of schooling, or all the sacrifices you might have to make in the beginning. Listen to this voice, if you must, but then let it leave you. Replace any negative thoughts with the rewarding feeling that will come when you reach your dream job or goal.

For some people, this is easy. You know you are an artist, or you know you are a musician, or you know you are an inventor. Maybe you lack the confidence it takes to step away from the norm and into your dream world. If it doesn't come easily, I want you to repeatedly ask yourself a hundred times a day, "What have I always wanted to do with my life?" Ask yourself at the coffee shop. Ask yourself while brushing your teeth. Ask yourself during the executive meeting in the office. Maybe you'll realize that you always wanted to run a coffee shop or bakery, or that you would be a great dentist. Maybe you'll discover that you should be the executive running that meeting. Define your dreams and then we'll look at how to make them happen.

Some people have found jobs that are sort of close to their dreams, but not really. Very few people make a living doing what they love. Why is that? You are here on this planet to express unique gifts and talents. You are a beneficial presence on this planet. The world needs you to be you. Your secret desires are the Universe's way of hinting at what you should be doing. It is ultimately your choice. Stop allowing fear to trap you in a job or situation you hate. It doesn't have to be this way. You can (and should) make a living doing what you are passionate about. Do not let any worry, doubt, or guilt get in the way of accomplishing *any* goal. It is your purpose here on Earth to live fully. It's your destiny. Your reason for living.

Imagine if you had all of the modern technologies available to you; yet you lived on a deserted island or the moon. For now, create a dream world. There can be people around you, but no one expects anything from you. Pretend you are obligated to no one but yourself. No one is asking you to turn in a report by a specific time. No one will ask you, "What's for dinner?" No one needs a thing from you. Let's just pretend that everyone else is taking care of themselves and all you have to do is focus on yourself. You are free to do whatever it is that makes you happy and at peace. What would you do with your time?

Maybe your fantasy lifestyle includes sitting around in pajamas, doing nothing, watching television. You probably think you need days like this to balance a week of working for someone else's dreams and goals. Maybe you've read these words so far and thought, "If I lived like that, I'd never get anything done!" Do you think that you would *remain* lazy if you could have freedom to own every day? How does that make you feel, to see yourself being unproductive? Eventually, you would get bored and you would do *something*.

Let's get to that place. What do you start doing? Gardening? Painting? Building? Running? Writing? Sewing? Shopping? Traveling? Reading? Maybe it's skydiving; maybe it's traveling to another country. Maybe you see yourself as a celebrity. Maybe it's wealth you're after and you see yourself owning a Fortune 500 company. A boat, a fast car, a gorgeous home, garden, exotic pet... Whatever passion speaks to your heart, that is what I want you to focus on. Imagine yourself doing that and having all of that, and pay attention to how that makes you feel. How does it feel to see yourself living out all of these dreams? How amazing is it that you conquered your fear and pursued your dreams? Doesn't it feel great? Isn't it a lot more fun to be *that* you, rather than the "couch potato" you?

I need you to know your answers. I am encouraging you to think about the answers to these questions after a deep meditation. I want you to think deeply about where you really want to be in your life. What did you always dream of doing? What secret desire have you always had but never gave attention to? Be specific *and* vague at the same time. We don't need to know the color of your dream car, but we should know that you've always wanted to drive and own a BMW 3 Series. We'll come back to these thoughts and expand on meditation exercises. I just have to plant the seed, so that you start to recognize that your secret yearning deserves your attention.

Another way to get answers is by asking yourself what you love. Let the answers be real and don't ever excuse them as being silly or unrealistic. The answers that seem unrealistic may be the ones that actually give you the most insight. You may find you always loved animals, or you love helping people and talking to people. Maybe you love magic and making balloon animals. What if (and do not allow any excuses to negate this answer) you could be doing what you love all day, every day? I'm here to tell you that you can. Start believing in yourself. Start believing in the reality of your dreams. No one can do that for you. You have to do this for yourself.

Think about how great you will feel being successful doing what you love. There is a personal joy that comes from fulfilling your dreams and goals. If your dreams and goals are to succeed as an executive director or manager in a large Fortune 500 company, you will be extremely fulfilled and happy when you reach that goal. Maybe your goal is to travel from the flea market to the estate sale, and to the auction house, in order to buy and sell antiques. When you find yourself doing that, you will be fulfilled and happy. The goal you set for yourself doesn't change the result you'll feel when you reach that goal. When we let society define our lives and goals and ambitions, we find ourselves feeling empty. We're tired at the end of the day, and all we want to do is relax and de-stress.

Next, ask yourself why you're not doing these things. Listen again to your answers. Do not beat yourself up or feel sorry for yourself. Don't allow yourself to make excuses. Your mind will tell you things like "rent," or "bills," or "my kids". This is resistance. These reasons trick your mind into living with complacency, and these excuses persuade you to be prisoner to your fears. When you take a stand for your dreams and for yourself, fear is squashed and diminished to nothing. You already know this. All of your great heroes laughed in fear's face. The only difference between these heroes and yourself is that you haven't yet stood up to fear and said, "Get out of my way! I have important things to do!"

One of my goals throughout high school and college was that by age 30 I wanted to be teaching art. After growing up, hearing adults say that being an "artist" was not a career, I thought I could at least become an art teacher (not that there is anything wrong with being an art teacher – I've just always wanted much, much more than that). At 28 years old, while waitressing in Chicago, I decided to peruse the classified ads for something artistic and creative. I found an ad for a part time after school art instructor. I immediately applied and got the job! I started out only working a couple of hours a week – I literally mean two hours per week at $18 an hour. That is a monthly salary of less than $150. Eventually I taught enough classes to reach an income of $3,000.00. For one year - $3,000.00.

Yet, I have never been so happy and fulfilled in my life! Not only was I amazed that I had completed a "life goal," but the job itself was so rewarding because it was never work! I enjoyed inspiring children. I enjoyed encouraging artists to see things in new ways. It taught me a lot about myself, and this job showed me how important it is to dedicate your life's work(s) to doing things you love. The money wasn't there, but the minimal hours allowed me to keep my waitressing job three nights a week (which averaged $100 a night). I was never without food or shelter. I had everything I needed, and I was happy with how I spent my time and talents.

When you are 82 years old and looking back on your life choices, are you going to say, "Wow! I did a lot of amazing things!" Or will you say, "I wish I had at least tried. I might have been able to do some really neat things had I only taken that first step." I don't know about you, but I want to say "Wow! I did a lot of really fantastic things that impacted a lot of people's lives. Life is *amazing!*"

One of the biggest differences between successful people and the mediocre, is that successful people believe in themselves. Successful people act on their instincts, and they rebel against society's standards when they feel their soul is suffering. The greater the rebellion, the greater the person. How many heroes do you know that live in the confines of a robotic job, or within the boundaries of society's standards? Why do we "put up" with things we internally disagree with, anyway? Is it because that submissive behavior deems us a "good person"? Conflict is simply the Universe saying to you, "Are you sure you wanna go on this ride? You have to be this tall." Your height is actually a measurement of confidence in yourself. Spectators watch people have fun on rides, while people who live life fully are enjoying themselves on the ride. Hop in, and let's go!

Your dream lifestyle *is* attainable. It doesn't matter where you are, or even how old or young you are. There is a way. You just have to find it. You have to seek it out, and take ownership of it. Take the recession, for example – a lot of 9 to 5-ers had to reassess their lives after being laid off. Some unemployed people found replacement 9 to 5 jobs, while others took advantage of the situation and started working for themselves. Not very many unemployed workers stayed in their pajamas, watching TV for the rest of their lives. Nobody really wants that. If you do desire this, you're probably so deep in the trap of working for others and neglecting your own dreams that you can't yet see how beautiful life can be when you are living for yourself.

There is really no certainty about your current job. It seems very secure because you *believe* that it's secure. You are surrounded by other people who believe the same thing. Coworkers also think that this is a stable lifestyle, so it must be true! You are choosing to believe that your regular job is safe and secure because you want to feel that feeling. What if you chose to believe that your dream job was safe and secure? What if you convinced your mind that your dream lifestyle is stable and secure? Do you see how both viewpoints are choices? Neither situation is a 100 percent guarantee of satisfaction, stability and security. We choose to believe society is secure, because we are surrounded by others who also choose to believe this is safe.

Imagine now what the result would be, if you surrounded yourself with people who believe in your real dream. Imagine if you put the same faith in your own goals and dreams. It could be true! Your dream can make you money. Your dream will be secure. Your dream will be certain. When you seek out your heroes, you will see that they are making money, paying all their bills, and sometimes even making more money than they were before they realized their dreams could come true. Most likely they are a thousand times happier, because they've made choices that utilize their true talent.

The greatest thing about pursuing your dreams and living your dream life, is that you will find that not only will you replace your income (and even exceed it), but you will have personal satisfaction and an inner peace that no amount of money can buy. You will find yourself so completely happy and at peace. You will be grateful to get up every day and work! When you choose to make your dream your career, you will be excited to wake up and start your day. You will want more. You'll want to create more, do more, be more and live more. Even if your current conventional job (that is not your dream) pays you a six figure salary, you may be missing out on this personal satisfaction and peace of mind.

A lot of resistance towards living your dream comes from a need to be financially stable. It is very valid as we all have bills, and we all have needs that must be met: clothing, food, traveling, transportation, etc. Should that stop you from challenging yourself? Should fear of lack of income be given enough weight that you don't ever pursue happiness? Think about something that you do during your day that is not productive. Maybe it is playing a computer game, watching a television show, going out to bars or clubs, or even reading before bed. Maybe it's making a trip to Starbucks or having a smoke break. I'm not going to suggest that you give up this habit completely. I want you to reduce it. Cut that time in half, and dedicate that amount of time to your dreams and goals. Do a little bit of something every day or at least every week. Take note at how your productivity rises, and see how far you can go in just a few months.

Then, look at your finances. Do you spend money on online gaming? What does it cost each month to have cable television? Answer *that* question in regards to time and money! How much money do you spend while out with friends for dinner or drinks? Cut unproductive spending in half for a few months and put it in a savings account. Do these two things together, and notice how you will have full control over your financial stability. The growth from these conscious changes may seem slow at first. Remember, by standing still and not doing anything – you will have gained nothing. In some cases, you may even move backwards by choosing to stand still.

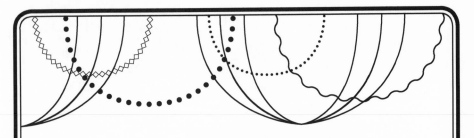

Fear stops people from pursuing dreams. It can be scary to initiate a change. It's unnerving to face possible rejection when asking for a raise, a better position or new tasks. It can be awkward to present a new, big idea to a boss, only to be laughed at or worse. It is so much easier to report to your station, and fly under the radar and keep your nose to the grindstone. But is it really worth it? Is this really how you want to spend your energy and your life?

Money will come. This is most people's biggest hindrance in pursuing their dreams. People find security and safety in a salaried job, a regular paycheck and structure defined by someone else. This is normal. This is mainstream thinking. The reality is that life is expensive and things cost money. But think about it. This is really a mentality that is feeding fear. "If I quit my office job, I'll lose my house." or "If I work a non-conventional job for myself, I could fail." What about all the successful people, doing what you'd love to be doing? Are they starving? Have they lost their homes? Or are they wealthy *and* happy?

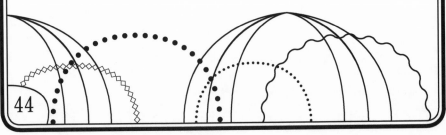

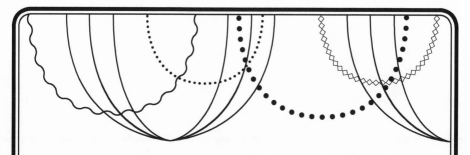

Whenever I thought about "how" I would work for myself, I would get discouraged about where the money would come from. I knew that as a business owner I would have to invest money, and that in the beginning I probably wouldn't make a very good return. There was never a clear answer for "how" I would be able to work for myself, on projects that I chose, during hours that were convenient for me.

I chose jobs that involved doing things I loved – but I was working for other people. I worked at print shops, designing newsletters and marketing material. I loved typography, design and promotions, but I did not enjoy designing junk mail. My art was literally being thrown in the trash! How shameful. Thankfully, I knew to ask myself an important question: "What would you rather be doing?" At this time in my life, my answer included society's standards of working for someone else. I worked many various art-related jobs, but none fulfilled my desire to be *The Artist, Rozine.*

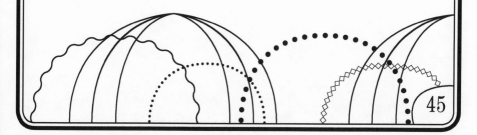

I realized that I needed to define my dream. I knew that I wanted to work for myself. I knew that I wanted to decide what projects I would be working on. I knew that I wanted to work from home so that I could create my own hours. I knew that I wanted to be known for my talents as a creative designer and artist, and I knew that I wanted to do big things. I knew these very basic things. I had no idea how I would do that and thinking about this "how" distracted me for years.

I started by simply believing that my dream was worth living. Then I began daydreaming. While in my cubicle at a corporate job, I would day dream about how lovely it would be to make my own schedule, and how amazing it would be to choose the jobs I wanted to work on. My imagination was very specific sometimes, and I would see myself working on a mural one week and in my then-fantasy studio, making glass mosaic art the next. It was so exciting to see myself in this imaginary place, instead of the reality where I was crunching numbers in spreadsheets that never ended.

Of course, fantasy lifestyles can only satiate someone for so long. Eventually, you have to decide to take action. You have to make a conscious choice and say to yourself, "Yes! I want this to happen!" Then you *really* have to take action. What good is a dream if it stays only in your imagination? First we define our dream. Then we decide to take action. And then, we truly take action.

No matter how exotic or unusual your dream is, there is a way to make a livelihood doing it. When you give your dream the same energy and focus that you give to your current job, you will be successful. It will provide for you. It might not fully replace your income at first, in which case you must simply balance it little by little alongside your day job, until eventually you are at a comfortable place that allows you to fully focus on your dream. Have faith in yourself, apply the tips I'm offering, and most importantly, believe that a gift was given to you to use in a way that will benefit you and the world.

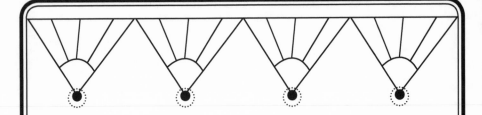

Don't expect to change your lifestyle overnight, and don't expect a magic wand to fall onto your lap that will make things easy for you. Do not get discouraged or depressed thinking about how much time you've already wasted. Instead, think about your dream, and strengthen it with a child-like imagination. Build that dream in your mind and heart until you want nothing else for yourself. The sooner you give your attention to your dreams, the sooner you will see results. The longer you procrastinate, the further you will find yourself from happiness. Isn't it wonderful? It's our choice! It's all up to us and our decisions! Let's get started!

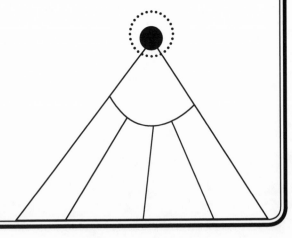

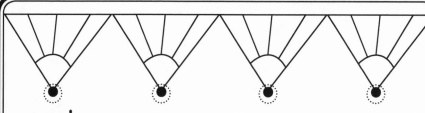

CHOICE

How do we do this? How did I go from working with never ending algorithms in gigantic spreadsheets, to living a very creative life with what appears to be a chaotic, random schedule and no routine? How did I build a life where words like "chaotic" and "random schedule" work to my advantage? Right now, I am at a place where I wake up to my own day. Sometimes I work on designing, and sometimes I work on writing. Sometimes I work on painting, and sometimes I make mosaics. I wake up when my eyes open, and not to an alarm.

There are times when I do work with others, and the projects that I'm working on sometimes demand that I wake up at 5am. However, it's never the same from day to day, or week to week. I create when I want, and what I want. I make a decision about every creative task I do. "Yes! I want to do this!", or "No, I think I'll pass." Though I may report to others (and I often do), I still choose the jobs that I want to do. How do you get to where you're making this type of decision for yourself?

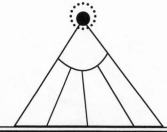

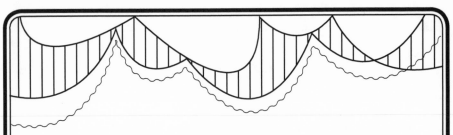

Start by simply visualizing and make a dream board. Meditate regularly to gain insight about your path and destiny. Clear some space in a room for your home office or work space. Gather supplies or inventory. Research other people and businesses in line with your goals and get familiar with the options available to you. We'll get to the details of each of those steps soon. There are simply too many lifestyle choices to define one way that will make it happen exactly for you. The foundation of *Live Life For A Living* applies to all dreams, but *you* have to make the definition. You'll know what it is that you can do right now.

Let's say you devoted one hour per day, or one task per day for ten years. At seven days a week, you'll have taken 3,650 steps (or hours) towards working for your dream, (not including leap years). Even if you only devote yourself to one task per week for ten years, you'll have accomplished over 500 tasks. If you are completely devoted to this idea and give "you" everything you have, you will be living your dream well before ten years have passed.

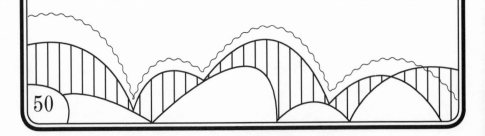

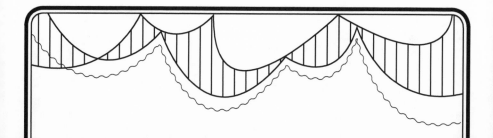

If you rebel against schedules, then don't force a routine. Find what is comfortable to you, and what it is that encourages you to stick to a path of making your dreams a reality. Encourage and develop self-discipline and devotion with the reward of dream fulfillment. Look at it as a sort of internship for yourself. "Your Dream" is the company that you're interning for, and it requires that you do what you can when you are available. Commit to doing something as often as you can.

Look at it this way. If you do nothing for ten years, you will be in the same place you are right now – longing for freedom and waiting for change. Maybe you'll have received a huge promotion or two, or even a career change – but you cannot reach a goal without first trying to get there.

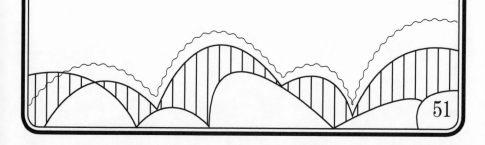

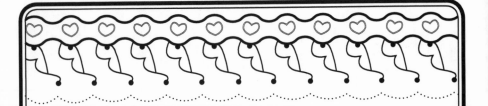

The sooner you start making things happen for yourself, the sooner you will see results. If you wait for the lottery, you'll find yourself looking back at a lot of wasted time. Look at that sentence. "If you *wait...*," you spend your life waiting. *Make* your life happen. *Make* your dreams come true. You are in control of your destiny, and you create your life. No one but you should dictate how you will live, or what you need to do to be happy. You have free will to make things happen for yourself. There are challenges, handicaps and limitations all over the world, and they are in every single person's life. They are not reasons to eliminate a dream. You'll see that once you reach your goals, those limitations, handicaps and challenges have disappeared and have actually become your strengths.

I needed to have brushes and paint in order to paint murals. I needed to have glass mosaics in order to make mosaics. I needed a way to offer my services to the public. Before I could physically do anything, I had to gather my tools and supplies. Fortunately for me, my corporate job was for an art supply company, and I had direct access to their outlet warehouse, as well as an employee discount.

On one trip to the warehouse, I saw an entire shelf full of glass mosaic tiles. They were selling for about 70% off the retail price. I looked at it and said to myself, "I want that whole thing." I didn't know what I was going to do with all that tile – it was a ridiculous amount of glass tile - but I knew that it was somehow important to my daydream/goal. I offered the clerk $100 for the entire shelf. They agreed, since the tiles had been sitting there, collecting dust for a while. I snagged $1,000 worth of glass mosaic tile for one-tenth of the price. I saw this as an opportunity to get closer to my dream life, and didn't allow any doubt or excuses to deter me.

I also collected brushes of various sizes, and spent any spare change that I had on my daydream/ goal. If I didn't have spare change, I used my time and talent to get me closer to my dreams. I have a graphic design background, and I designed business cards, postcards and even a website to advertise and promote my skills and abilities. I did this at nights and on the weekends while working in a cube, crunching numbers Monday-Friday, 9 to 5. The point is that I took steps. I took big risks – $1,000 worth of tiles is heavy and takes up a lot of space! I took baby steps – a brush here, two brushes there. I talked about my daydream/goal and made it more real every single day.

I applied the same work ethic that I applied to my corporate job, and gave myself and my daydream/goal the same energy. I worked double shifts for about a half of a year. One shift for the corporation, and then another four to eight hours for myself. I worked every night and even on weekends. I did this until I was able to walk away from the corporation and work solely for myself every single day. It took determination, dedication, passion and a strong will. If I found myself doubting my efforts, I would think about my reward. You have to be careful how you perceive your progress. Baby steps result in stepping stones, which add up to a dramatic response over a long period of time. Giant leaps can result in dramatic responses more quickly, but the risk is also greater. Recognize your progress for what it is and see how it is getting you closer and closer to success each day.

One of my fears about quitting my corporate job was, of course, the financial security it gave me. I wasn't making as much money doing my artistic jobs as I was in the 9 to 5 job, and I feared that I would be without work (and money) after quitting. What I actually found was that as soon as I made time for more artistic endeavors, more artistic jobs came my way! My income was easily replaced by new income. Why? Because no matter where I was or what I was doing, the fact was that I was getting paid to show up and work. Here we have a choice again. Should I show up and work for someone else's dream and get paid for something I don't enjoy doing? How about if I show up to my own dream life, do something that I love, and get paid for that?

I have not had a regular paycheck since leaving the corporation. I have not repeated the same artistic endeavor since walking away from the corporation. I've painted murals, designed sets, and sold graphics on t-shirts, skateboards and shoes. I've created websites and I've written this book. I've done things that I never had time for when I worked for someone else. I have been able to pay my bills. I have explored many amazing creative endeavors. I have grown as an artist. I make my own schedule, and decide when I want to take a day off and go to the beach.

By facing and overcoming a fear, I made another dream come true! I am doing something that existed only in my imagination for many years. I was learning that if I defined what I wanted, and then decided to take action towards that thing, and then actually took steps towards fulfilling my desires, I could in fact live my dreams! I made my own dreams come true. See? You just read how easy it is! I didn't have to take out a loan or wait for a miracle to happen. I just defined my dreams and then decided to take action, and then I took action!

Before you know it, you will be doing more and more things related to your goals. You'll realize how much you love doing these things. You will not be able to get enough of it. Time will transform. When you are doing what you love, the eight hours of torture you felt while at your place of employment will soon feel like only an hour or two.

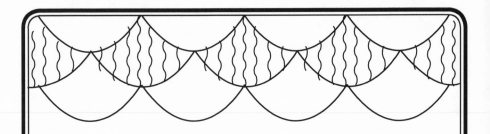

Of course, this random, chaotic and creative lifestyle is not for everyone, and I don't want you to feel excluded if you are not interested in such choices. You can apply the same logic for your own daydream/goals. The principle is the same. If your daydream/goal is to be the Vice President of the corporation you work at, you can daydream about the goal until you are certain about what it is you want. Then you can decide to take action. Then you can take action towards that daydream/goal and eventually, with baby step after giant leap after baby step, you will reach your goal.

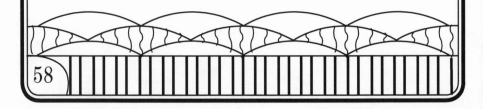

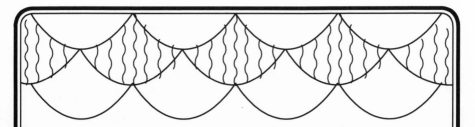

Seek out people that have the same dream as you. Find examples of successful people who are living the dream you want to have. There are plenty of people in the world already doing what you want to be doing. I guarantee it. No matter how unique or unconventional you think your dream might be, someone is already doing it somewhere in the world, and they are successful at it. Did you know that people make a living from knitting? There are people who travel the world, taking photographs of everything that is beautiful, and they are getting paid for it!

Think about it. People are doing these things that seem so farfetched in the mind. It only seems farfetched because you're not already doing it. What about those that are successful at doing the thing that is your dream? Is it far fetched for them? No! They are *doing* it. They are living that dream that you want to be living. Find them. Seek them out. Follow them. Read about them, watch them, and learn from them. If you're lucky enough to ask them questions about how they did what they are doing, ask them! Let them mentor you, even if only from afar.

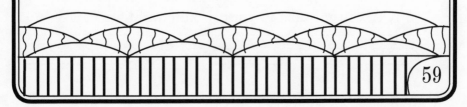

Find your personal heroes and study them. This is the information age, and people's lives and lifestyles are easily accessed online. Try to research how your hero got to where they are today. Find their "way," and let it inspire you. Realize that it can be done and it is being done. If your heroes are accessible, interview them. Ask them questions that will help erase your fears. Let them explain their hardships and their happiness. People love to talk about themselves, and if you listen with an open mind and an open heart, you'll learn very valuable lessons without having to go through all of the personal experiences yourself.

Don't get bitter or jealous about other people's success and life fulfillment. Maybe you had a poor upbringing and your hero was born with a silver spoon, and that was how they are able to fulfill their dreams and life path. Take what you can from that hero, and then find another person who is living the dream but with a harder upbringing, or something more like your own life story. The more people you seek out, the better variety you will find. You'll learn that you are not alone in your dream. You will see that others have battled the same fears and challenges, and are happily living their dreams. There is enough opportunity in the world to supply us all with a dream and happiness. There are a million ways to make it happen, but only if you partake in your dream and life goals.

Surround yourself with loving and supportive people. Take a close look at the people who are in your daily life. Those who are not supportive, or who try to convince you that your dreams are illogical and unreal, are not interested in your happiness. You know who these people are. You feel disappointed, ashamed, and uninspired after chatting with them. You do not need to make these people your priority anymore. You can be there for them when and if they reach out to you. Put yourself first. If you do choose to put others before yourself, make sure you really want to be suffering for this person or cause. Remember that it is your choice.

Make supportive, encouraging and inspiring people your new best friends. These are the people who are going to cheer for you, regardless of their own objectives. You will want to seek out and surround yourself with good people from now on. Reassess your companions and friends. Not in a materialistic or demeaning way. Pay attention to how a person adds value or enhances your life. Once you recognize the discouraging people, you can slowly release your obligation to them. They have chosen a different journey than your own and that is their free will, as it is yours to choose your journey.

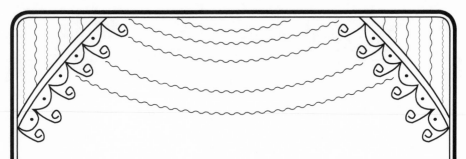

Judging a person based on material things or cosmetic qualities will not benefit anyone, including yourself. Instead, pay attention to people's behavior. Are your friends using you? Are your coworkers abusive? Are people telling you your dreams are unrealistic? Or, are they encouraging you to be happy and healthy? Are they listening to your dreams with excitement and anticipation? Are they supporting you by lending advice, or pointing you in directions that help you succeed?

This is the type of assessment you should apply to the people surrounding you. If you don't know any supportive people, seek them out. Listen to strangers and talk to them. You'll recognize the good, supportive people after asking yourself the questions above. You'll know a person of value from a naysayer by the way they treat the people they are surrounded by. Make friends with strangers, until you find yourself surrounded by people who are supportive, encouraging and willing to listen to your dreams. Don't be shy — introduce yourself and give compliments. Seek out inspirational people, websites, and resources. Find the encouragement and motivation you need. Make this a daily part of your life.

You have a choice. You have millions of choices to make. Let's take two opposing personalities: a pessimist (we'll call him Paul), and an optimist (we'll call her Olivia). Paul and Olivia are going to the movies and there is a long line. The waiting becomes even longer when the ticket taker's machine freezes. Paul the Pessimist starts complaining and grumbling about how terrible this is, and how he's going to miss the movie and that waiting in line sucks. Olivia the Optimist, on the other hand, does not lose patience. She looks around at people in the theater, smiles at the smell of popcorn and looks forward to seeing the movie. She is glad to be out. She is proud of the human race for creating such a thing as a movie theater. She thinks about, and is grateful for the people who dedicate themselves to the magic of movie making, just so that she can have an hour or two of entertainment.

They are both in the same line, with the same circumstances in front of them. Neither person has any idea how long they will be waiting, or whether they will even be let into the theater. One person is in agony, while the other is at peace.

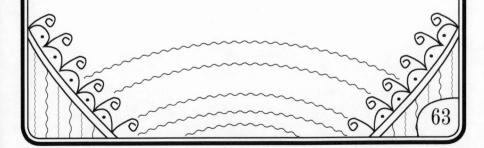

Was Paul the Pessimist handed a different set of cards to play with? Was Olivia the Optimist given something to keep her happy while in line? The thing to pay attention to in this example is that each person made a choice about their circumstances. Each person chose their destiny. One chose to be negative, while the other chose to be at peace. You can choose to be happy. You can choose to pursue your dreams. You can choose to live the life you've always wanted to live.

Maybe you have some limitations, challenges or handicaps. You can choose to let them deter you from pursuing whatever it is that makes you happy. You can blame the world for making things difficult for you and live a bitter and unfulfilled life, or you can choose to overlook those challenges and remain determined to see your dreams come true. Here we have the same circumstance with two different choices. Hopefully now you see that there are nothing but excuses to back up your "I can't do that" voice. You can do anything, and you should do everything that makes you a joyful, happy person.

Oprah Winfrey is a wonderful example of how overcoming challenges leads to greatness. She was born into poverty to a teenage single mother, in urban Milwaukee. Nothing about the beginning of her life says "she is destined to be great!" How many poor, black women in an urban, ghetto environment do you know achieve great things? We all know the impact Oprah has made on the world. Her determination to succeed is admirable and inspirational.

Lance Armstrong's health hurdles show us that nothing will stand in the way of a determined dreamer. Our heroes have devoted their lives to being wonderful. Even heroes face challenges and have to overcome personal hardships. Fear is a common emotion that exists in every life form. What humans have that most other lifeforms don't have is the free will to choose. That means that our destinies are in our own hands. We can attempt to live a full life or we can choose to sit on the sidelines and watch others live full lives.

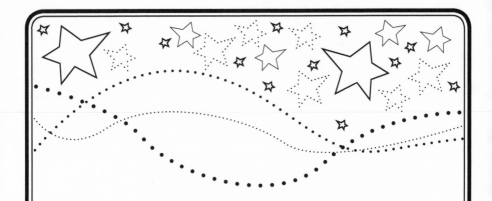

One key to the success of living your dreams is flexibility. If you are rigid and close-minded, it may be difficult for you to see your dreams come true. Flexibility is a quality that can truly benefit you. Things happen in our lives that are out of our control. If we are inflexible during these moments, we won't be able to overcome the event, and we will waste precious time and energy in conflict. If we remain open and flexible to life and its circumstances, we will move with grace and ease through every event.

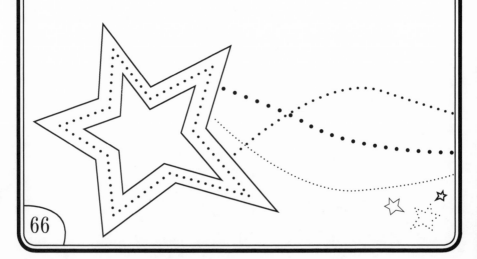

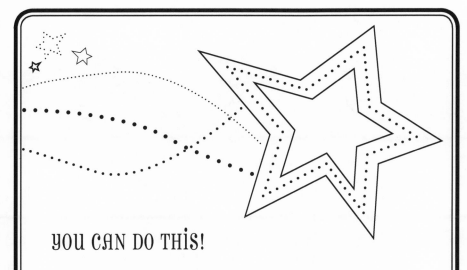

YOU CAN DO THiS!

I want you to try and remove all mental blocks to your success. How do you do that? Change the way that you think about your dream lifestyle. When you start to daydream about your true happiness, allow yourself to really see it in its full potential. Really see how productive you are. See yourself as so completely successful. Realize how happy this vision makes you feel. Imagine feeling so full of joy and amazement. I don't really have to lead your feelings here. I know that when you think about living your dream fully, every day, that you feel amazing and happy and successful. Feel that way. Allow yourself that happiness in your heart. Let it fill your mind, body and soul.

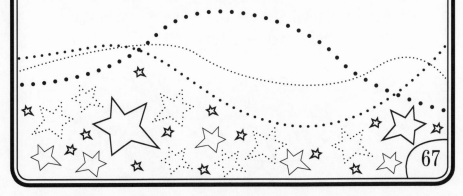

I know you are probably thinking of all the reasons why your dream is a bad idea. I bet these reasons are short term – meaning they are issues for the first few months of a transition period between your current lifestyle and your dream life. I need you to get past that. Just for this one moment, I need you to pretend like these reasons are not real. Believe that they are made up and focus only on the end result of living life for a living.

Once you have released all of the mental blocks that hold you back from fulfilling your dreams and goals, you will fully and truly believe in yourself. You will know that you are a unique individual. You have a set of talents that are unique to you. Believe in *your* talent! Do not in any circumstance undermine it or take it for granted. You are here on this planet with a gift unique to you, and even if another person also has that gift, you will express yourself uniquely and reach a different group of people. Acknowledge that the world needs your talent, and believe fully in that gift.

As I've mentioned already, I felt deeply that I was an artist from a very young age, and nothing could ever change that. I had a very deep belief in my gift. I did not always believe in my talent, though. For a very long time, I struggled with believing in my talent, because I would step back and look at my art work and think that it was nothing like I had imagined it would be. I would get frustrated at my primitive artwork, and would think I was such an amateur.

However, since I believed in my *gift* as an artist, I knew I would one day create artwork that would be amazing, even though my early work was childish. Had I instead looked at my artwork and said, "Well, it looks like my work is not what I expected. I should just give up. It will always be terrible and I'll never get any better," I would not be where I am today. You tell me how that statement would ever bring me to a place where I was creating amazing artwork. It never would!

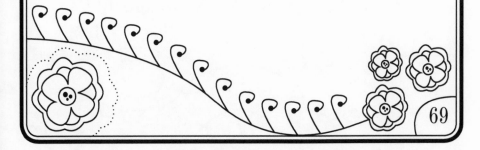

Believing that although I was not great at the time, but one day I would be, easily led me to a place where now, as an adult, people watch me paint in awe. I'm hired to create graphics, and my clients are always impressed. It comes so easily to me now that I make it look like magic when I create. I believe in my talents, my gifts, my unique vibration and combination of characteristics and qualities.

The world wants you to be productive. The world needs you to be *you*. The world wants and needs you to live to your full potential. That is why people who live big have big things. I don't mean necessarily big physical things. People who live fully are known and respected, called upon and admired. Think about someone you admire. Maybe it is an actor or an inventor. It could be a relative, friend or coworker. Think about why you admire them. They most likely did something huge or gutsy. If they can do it, why can't you? You *can*! Once you do start doing huge, gutsy things, you will reap great rewards and you will laugh at the fears you used to have that hindered you from moving forward.

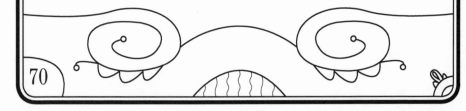

Let's look at famous actors, musicians, and artists. Those are obvious examples of people that wake up every day and chose their dream. They didn't put it on hold and tell themselves they couldn't do it. We admire successful people, but we don't think we can do it ourselves. Why should we let other people chase their dreams, while we sit back and watch them on television? We all deserve to experience life to the fullest.

If you ever doubt yourself or worry about the "what if's", change your mind. Change your thinking. Challenge that fear. Were you ever afraid of something only to realize that it really wasn't so bad? I remember being afraid to ride my bike no-handed. I had convinced myself that if I let go of the handle bars while riding, that I would surely fall over instantly. I thought that by riding no-handed, the bike would topple over, or wave back and forth violently out of control. Thankfully, I challenged that fear-voice, and reminded myself that I had seen my brothers ride no-handed with effortless ease and grace. They did not fall over, nor did they swerve all over the place uncontrollably.

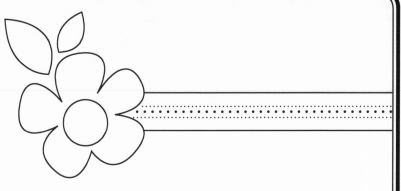

I attempted riding my bike without holding on to the handle bars. At first, it was in fact swerving all over the place, but that was because my mind and my thoughts were dictating that it should be. My lack of confidence translated into little control over the bike. I kept trying and did not give up. Eventually, it did work. I did not fall, and the more I practiced, the better I got at it. After a very short while, I was a pro at riding bike no-handed and it was exhilarating! It was so cool! I could even drink water while riding my bike. I was so confident that I could even go around corners no handed! I was steering the bike with my force of energy! I changed my mind about how I felt about the situation, and I conquered the fear I had about the circumstances and succeeded!

I want you to apply this same logic to your dream lifestyle. Acknowledge your fear. Challenge it. Practice living without fear, and enjoy the exhilaration from succeeding at your goal! Trust that you were given abilities that are valuable, which are meant to be used to their fullest potential. Believe that you are capable, ready and willing to do what you're meant to do. Take action towards your goals and be passionate about your dreams. All three of these things erase fear. Fear makes you weak while trust, belief and action are strengths.

Fear is not an acceptable answer. Fear inhibits you from fully being yourself. You are here on this planet to add value, and fear is a trick of the mind that allows bad bosses (and parents) to have control over you to do what they want you to do. It has its place and is a necessary life force – but you don't have to let it rule your life. Recognize that fear is there. Pay attention when you feel fear and call it out. After a while, you'll naturally laugh at fear and it will no longer control your life. You'll soon be saying, "I can't believe I let that jerk boss me around and talk to me like that!" You'll know that you deserve better, and that your time and energy is valuable and should be used for *you* – not anyone else.

Once you start doing the things you love, fears and anxious worries will dissolve, and you will realize how much you love being *you*! You will be able to laugh in the face of fear and say, "So what? It's worth it!" In other words, the fears will not seem so huge that they stop you from pursuing your dream. You will instead be seeing the reward that comes from being who you really are.

If you have taken the steps to break free from others' demands, and you have defined your own demands for your own life, you will start to notice a change. If you have taken steps towards noticing your gut feelings and paying attention to your surroundings, you will also see a change. You're listening and communicating better, and your mind is working more efficiently. You'll find that you are always on time, while never needing to wear a watch. You'll always be prepared without making lists. You will just know what needs to happen and when.

I'm not asking you to change the world necessarily, unless of course that is your life's dream and desire. I'm asking you to change your own thinking and behavior. You have a life to live on this planet, and you have been given gifts and wondrous amounts of luck. You have been given the right to choose how you want to live your life. You can choose to work as a waitress, or 9 to 5 in a cube, or you can choose to live every day as if it was your own. You can own every day. It's yours to do with as you please — not what anyone else wants, but what *you* want. It's not being selfish. It's not about being a punk just to rebel. It's about living your life fully, and with passion about who you are. It's about expressing your true self, and living your true meaning.

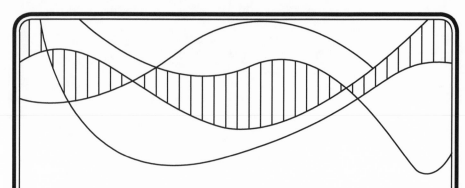

Look at it this way. Most of us have a car. It is probably not the same car that everyone in your neighborhood has. Maybe a few people you know have the same car, but it could be in a different color, or with different options. We very easily choose to get a car that speaks to us personally, and on some level becomes a statement about our personalities. Imagine if everyone drove the same exact car — same model, same year, same color. You know that is not attractive, so why should your lifestyle choices be any different? If you want the bright orange car because you desire to stand out in the crowd, buy the bright orange car. If the silver VW Jetta speaks to you; even if half the neighborhood drives the same car, get the silver VW Jetta. Use the same selfish drive that determines your car choice to decide your career path and lifestyle. If you want to do nothing but paint and show art in a gallery, paint away!

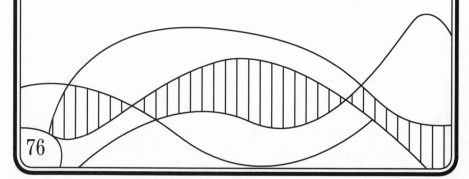

There isn't just one rule that applies to every lifestyle or dream. What this encouragement and wisdom can offer is inspiration and guidance, so you can start to pursue what you've always *really* wanted to do. If you are already a loyal, hard-working employee who is determined to please your boss and work forty hours a week with little to no complaints, you're a step ahead of the game. Apply those same qualities, ethics and energies to yourself and your own dreams. If you're reading this, you are already desiring to do something and you're looking for a little extra push to tell you "you can do this," well... ***you can do this!***

You don't even need to have a physical place of business anymore. You can work online from your house or a coffee shop. There are a plethora of industries and outlets that encourage, support and produce non-conventional employment. If you like to buy and sell antiques, there is eBay. If you are an artist, there are sites like Etsy, Zazzle and ArtFire, to name a few among many. If you're a photographer, you can sell your photos for royalties at sites like iStock Photo. If you're an athlete, you can become a personal trainer or instructor. You can advertise services like accounting, landscaping, home repair work, child care, and even legal services on many classified sites. Check your local newspaper, or even physically "pound the pavement." Talk about your goals everywhere you go to everyone you see. The possibilities are endless.

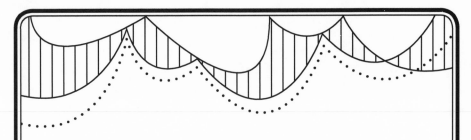

You know this is true. You see others living their dreams. You see others around you happy and fulfilled. You might think they are lucky or that they know some secret, or were given some gifts that you don't have. But those are lies. You are lucky. You have gifts, too! The reason people you see happy are fulfilled is because they believe in themselves. They use their gifts, and they know they are lucky. What they have available is available to you, too. Are you thinking, "I have a family to think about and they don't," or "they have extremely rich parents and I don't"? These things are false beliefs. It doesn't matter what they have and you don't, or what you have and they don't. There are people worse off than you who are making their dreams come true. You have the same gifts as every other person. You are just as lucky as the extremely rich child. You have just as much strength as the wheelchair bound athlete. You have just as much hope as the terminally ill patient.

Trust yourself. Believe in yourself. Give energy to your passion.

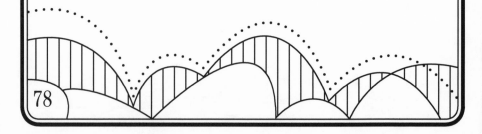

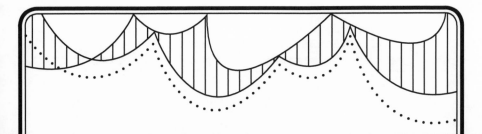

guide to meditation

Whether or not you are aware of it, you already know how to meditate. You do it on a daily basis. For example, whenever you're doing a mundane task, like brushing your teeth or taking a shower, you are thinking. Your mind is wandering and you allow your thoughts to drift off to some place other than where you physically are. This is meditation. When you do this consciously, you can gain great insights about yourself and your life.

Find a space that is free of distractions. Ideally the place should be comfortable and worry free. Try to find somewhere that doesn't have any to-do tasks (like cleaning, fixing or remodeling). A nice warm bath can be a great escape if you have no other private sanctuary space in your home. Consider a quiet and undisturbed outdoor area if that speaks to you. You might even want to sit in your car – if that's the only place free from kids, roommates, chores and distractions.

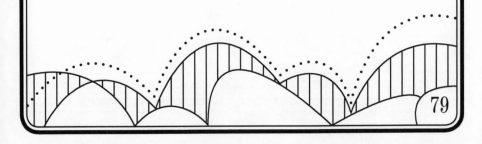

Get really comfortable. Grab a pillow, a blanket and maybe even some incense. Sit or lie on the floor, couch, or chair. Play some soft, calming music (preferably without any lyrics). Be completely still in your body and mind. Thoughts will try to race through your mind and that is natural. Don't fight it. Let them come and go. Watch your thoughts fly by. By practicing this exercise on a regular basis, you'll overcome the distractions and master being still.

I find that when I lie on the floor or on a bed, completely still, I am able to find the most peace. One exercise I do to quiet my mind, involves an invisible blanket. I start at my toes and imagine this blanket lifting up over my feet. As it passes my ankles, I feel that my feet are completely relaxed. I lift the blanket higher over my legs, towards my knees and again, as it passes over me, each body part relaxes and becomes completely still.

If you find that your mind starts to drift or wander and you've forgotten where the blanket last was, start over at your feet. Simply try the exercise again. Move slowly up your body and notice that your breathing becomes deeper, and you feel more and more relaxed. The racing thoughts will start to vanish as you pull the invisible blanket higher over your body. With your mind's eye, pull it up over your thighs, hips and waist. Let your body relax as you include your fingertips, hands, wrists and arms. Concentrate on bringing the blanket up over your chest and shoulder blades.

When you get to this point, you should feel almost as if your body is floating. Your body should feel light, relaxed and free of tension. You mind will be clearer than it was before you started the exercise. You may even fall asleep. Stay with this stillness as long as you can. If you're ready to go further and deeper into meditation, you'll let your body rise up out of where you are sitting or lying. This is a form of an out-of-body experience that can easily be mastered if you are ready and willing.

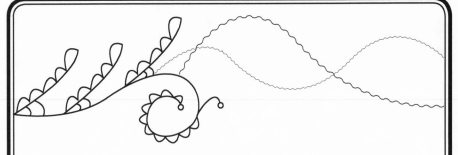

With your imagination, float up out of the building you're in. Float high above the trees and look down over the city where you live. Look up above you and float even higher. Float above the clouds and look back down at the earth as if you are in the Space Station. Keep going deeper and deeper into space until you can't feel your body anymore. You will sense that you are now simply a source of energy; a wisp of smoke; a fluff of a cloud. You may find yourself twirling, dancing or even what feels like swimming through space. This is a wonderful place to be. Stay here for a moment and just be with yourself. Find the peace and quiet you desire, and notice how you feel and what you're thinking about. You should be able to ask yourself some very serious questions that confused you in the physical realm of Earth. The answers will be clear and may seem very obvious. Take note at what you see, hear and feel here and bring it back with you when you return to your body.

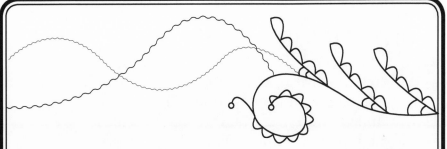

There is yet another deeper level of meditation that goes beyond floating in space above Earth. If you look far beyond where you are swimming, past the sun and all of our solar system, you will see a bright, pure, white light that is the center of our galaxy. Like a moth to a lightbulb, once you spot it you will be drawn to it. If you feel comfortable, let yourself go towards the light. It will take little effort at this point, as you have already brought yourself very far into a deep state of meditation. Once you reach the light, you may feel you are being hugged by pure love. It should feel safe, warm, inviting and comfortable. When I have gone this far into meditation, I have found that the questions in which I thought were very critical to my life on Earth, are silly and petty in comparison to the wisdom and knowledge that exists in this bright, pure light. I find that I return to my body feeling a tremendous amount of love and compassion for every living being on the planet. I find that my troubles are non-existent compared to the amount of blessings in my life.

DREAM BOARD

A dream board is a visual reference to remind you what's important. Sometimes dream boards are compiled on refrigerator doors or cubicle walls without our intention. We subconsciously gather things that make us smile and feel good and put them on display. That way, if we're having a hard day we can glance over at our reminders and smile and feel good.

An intentionally made dream board does the same thing. The difference is that our refrigerators and cubicle walls usually show us things we already have, or people we already know. A dream board is made up of the things you wish to acquire and attain. For example, my current dream board shows a book with the title *Live Life For A Living*. You're reading this, so that means I've accomplished that goal. The book didn't always exist. I made a habit of visualizing the completion or attainment of the things on my dream board. I have a printed out hard copy of my dream board hanging on the wall. Every time I walk by it, I see this book completed and I'm motivated to make that dream come true. I also have a digital version of my dream board as my wallpaper on my laptop screen so that every time I look at my desktop, I am reminded of my goals.

There are several other items on my dream board, too. I have a picture of an outdoor work space that has a canvas canopy and comfortable seating, a fire pit, and beautiful plants and flowers. Another picture shows a garage or workshop filled with what looks like junk. To me, I see gallons of paint, tools, work tables, paint brushes, old furniture that I'm refurnishing, and tons of glass and ceramic for mosaic arts. Another image shows my name with the IMDb logo, along with a few Art Department credits. This is another goal that I have attained. When I added this image, I didn't have very many IMDb credits. Since that time, I have accumulated several.

I have a graphic that shows my income from my Zazzle and ArtFire stores as six-digit numbers. There is an image of a woman doing a difficult yoga pose, which I'm getting better at every time I try it. There's a bird's eye view floor plan of my dream house, and a picture of a happy couple leisurely walking hand in hand down a cafe lined boulevard.

All of these images invoke some kind of motivation in me. Every picture shows me what I want in my life. I found these images online using search engine results for things that were important to me. I've encouraged you to know you – now you can utilize your new skills. Go online, or use magazines that interest you, and find images of the things you want to have in life. Do not skimp here! Do not allow yourself to underestimate what you could have. Maybe you'd love a specific diamond necklace, but your mind says, "You can't afford that! You'll never be able to afford that!" Quiet that voice and save that image of the diamond necklace!

Think of physical things that you can attain, like the necklace, a car, a swimming pool, a new addition to the house, or your art hung in a museum. Find images that make you feel deeply. Select the pictures that make you feel in your gut, "I want *that*!" Collect images of things you want to be. For instance, some words you could use would be healthy, wealthy, inspirational, magical, famous, respected. You can use words, graphics, images or photographs. I really can't tell you what to use – because again, *you* know *you*.

Gather all of these images. Place them into a document or file that allows you to place and arrange such photos. Make it pretty, so that you really want to look at it every day. We want this collage to inspire and motivate you. Make sure that it does those things. If you're using magazine clippings, glue them to another piece of paper, and hang it where you'll see it every day. Print out the graphic if you've done this exercise virtually. Put it as your desktop image, too. You may find that you need to replace things as they come true. You may even remove things if after time you decide that they aren't really what you want.

That is just step one. The next step is visualizing. It is very critical to pay close attention to the advice given here about visualization. Look at each image separately. Let the meaning of each goal fill your mind, heart and body. Think of it as if you already have it. Do not in any circumstances let yourself think about this thing in a future tense. If you do that, you are only telling your mind that you'll have it in the future – but the future will never come. It will always be tomorrow. It sounds weird, but when you visualize the "thing" as if it already exists in your life – it will get closer to you every day.

Of course, it is highly unlikely that the dream will materialize before your eyes (although that has been known to happen). Visualizing will attract things to you. Dreaming about already having something encourages your subconscious to make decisions throughout the day that bring you closer to those items.

Let's take this book, for example. I look at my dream board and see a hard cover book with a dust jacket that reads "*Live Life For A Living* by Lynnette Rozine Prock". I think to myself "yea, one day, maybe I'll write that book." And then, what happens? I don't take any daily action to write the book because nothing is motivating me to do it today. I'll do it some future date (which never comes). If instead, I look at that same image and think, "How cool is that I have a published book? People are buying it. It's flying off the shelves, and I have an interview tomorrow to discuss its success." Now, I have this inner desire and motivation to get busy and start writing.

Odd things will happen when you visualize on a regular basis. You'll notice some things you never thought possible will start appearing on your door step. Opportunities will come to you from nowhere. One of the many pictures on my dream board includes a funky theater set design that I thought looked neat. I always wanted to paint back drops for theater stages. I wasn't actively seeking this type of work, but I would certainly visualize about how I would feel to participate at a theater in this capacity. The image sitting right above this funky theater set design was of an outdoor wall mural painted by children with the supervision of adults. Another interest I wanted to pursue.

Neither of the images reflected exactly what I wanted to do. The funky stage design was elaborately constructed. It didn't show intricately painted backdrops. The childrens' mural was not even my style of art. Still, both pictures sparked some kind of deep seeded desire to participate. While I have several things on my dream board, for some time, these two spoke loudest to me. With some of the other images, I would have to concentrate really hard in order to see myself having it. But for a few weeks, as soon as I looked at these two images, my eyes got big, and I got excited. I was ready to go.

89

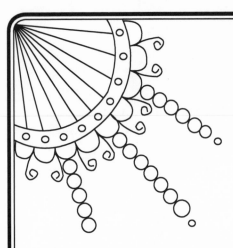

Soon after that, a good friend emailed me a listing he saw on a classified post. It was for a theater nearby that was looking for someone to paint back drops for a child's play. Out of nowhere, the thing that I visualized doing was about to happen! Try it for yourself. If you find that nothing is coming your way, re-assess the way you are thinking about the images. Do you feel in your heart that those things are with you right now, or that they are coming your way? Or is your mind filled with doubt while visualizing? It doesn't do a bit of good to visualize unless you *believe* that you already have it.

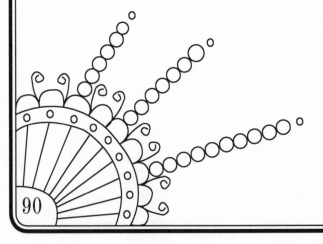

AFFIRMATIONS

Affirmations can help you develop self esteem and confidence that leads to personal growth. You can change the way you perceive yourself, when you repeat a statement over and over again. This works for both positive and negative statements. By reminding yourself each day how beautiful, great and essential your existence is, you raise the expectations of yourself. It may not be obvious at first, but affirmations gradually motivate you to make better, more meaningful decisions throughout the day.

For example, when you state that you can't cook, you reaffirm this belief. It is just a belief. You can cook. Anyone can cook if they try. It might take fifty tries before you make something that is delicious, but the truth is you have the ability to cook. By stating that you can't cook, you are allowing yourself the excuse not to try. Why should you try? You already know you can't cook! Start saying that you can cook, or at least say you'll *try*. Just by stating that you can, you've given yourself permission to try. You've removed old excuses and opened doors that lead to new opportunities and successes.

Another way to look at the power of saying affirmations is an example of outside reinforcement. When your parent, child or partner says "I love you," you feel that love instantly. You may already know that they love you, but when it is verbalized, you're reminded and the feeling is brought to the forefront of your life. You feel it right away. When you hear "I love you" every day by people who matter to you, you know without a doubt that you are loved. If a loved one hasn't told you they love you in awhile, you might start to wonder if they've lost love for you. As soon as they remind you, you know instantly and you remove all prior doubt. The same thing happens when you say affirmations. You remind yourself that *you* love *you*. By repeating positive statements, you remove doubt that may have been building up inside. When you repeat affirmations on a daily basis, your confidence becomes stronger.

I offer free affirmations online at my website www.MyDreamsMatter.com/affirmations/. Purchase and download audio versions and repeat them after me. Or, simply read them from the website. There are other resources available if these don't speak to you the way you need them to. You can also create your own affirmations. I highly recommend this, as you know best what you need to hear.

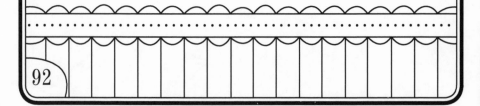

Start by using this format to list all the things you want to have and be:

I want to have _____

I want to be _____

I want to give _____

Some examples may be:

I want to have a clean bill of health.
I want to have a happy family.
I want to have a million dollars.

I want to be healthy.
I want to be happy.
I want to be a millionaire.

I want to give encouragement to my family
to be healthier.
I want to give my family a happy home.
I want to give to charity.

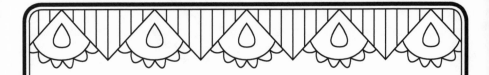

All of those statements are in a future tense. It's easier to start this way, because we know what we want since we don't currently have it. Similarly to visualizing, affirmations only work when you state clearly that you already have or do these things. The next step, then, is to turn these statement into present tense.

I have a clean bill of health.
I have a happy family.
I have a million dollars.

I am healthy.
I am happy.
I am a millionaire.

I give encouragement to my family
to be healthier.
I give my family a happy home.
I give to charity.

Just like visualizing, affirmations must be said with conviction. Repeat the sentences with strong will and a strong voice. Picture what you're saying as if it already is that way. You *are* a millionaire. You *are* happy and healthy. You may not see instant results. It might take a great amount of time to see anything. If it's not working at all, you may be letting doubt, worry or fear into the exercise. Your belief in the statement is what makes it true.

If you're not used to repeating affirmations on a daily basis, it can feel strange at first. The more you do it and the more regular you are, the quicker you'll experience more confidence and self esteem. Take it slowly, and really visualize what each statement means. Envision yourself at that place where the statement takes you. See yourself already as you want to be. By doing this, you remind yourself of hidden, buried potential within yourself. Remembering these qualities will trigger new decisions in your day to day life that will lead to bigger and better things.

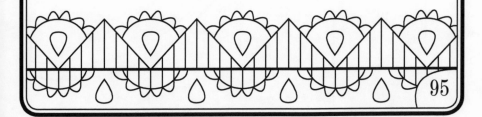

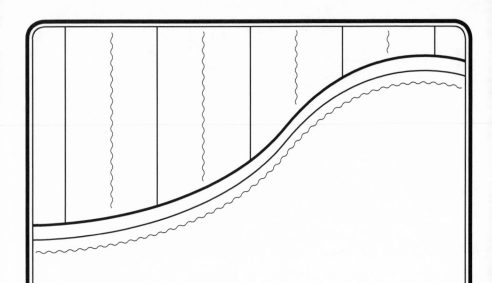

GOALS

We've learned extensively about defining your dreams. You've meditated, visualized and repeated affirmations. Where's the progress? It's hard to see how far you've come if there are never any established goals. You can go on the rest of your life meditating, visualizing and saying affirmations with little to no results if you haven't established any goals.

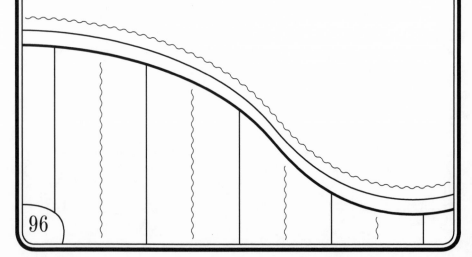

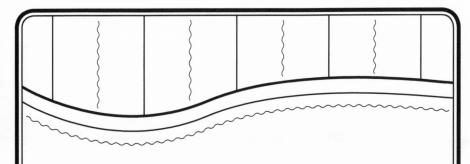

We need to have some destinations to reach or else we will find ourselves aimlessly drifting with only good intentions. Large goals can be intimidating, and small goals can turn into distractions. We need to find a balance of both long and short term goals that collectively bring us to our dreams. I've created a worksheet for your guidance. I've incorporated meditation, affirmations and visualizing exercises to keep you on track. You can also download (for free) a more stylized version online at www.MyDreamsMatter.com. Check off that you've meditated, visualized and repeated your affirmations - daily. Answer a few short questions about each exercise to give you ideas about where you've grown and what you need to work on. List your ideal goals for the day, week, month and year. Reflect on what you actualized yesterday, last week, last month and last year. Even if your progress is minor, you'll see that it exists. With that motivation, you can boldly continue to make your dream a reality.

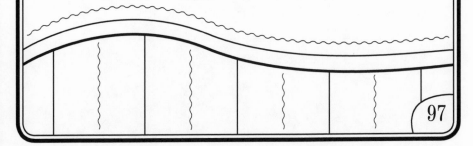

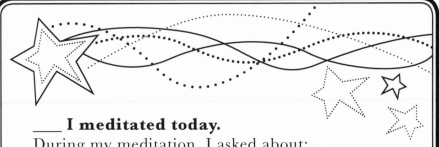

___ I meditated today.

During my meditation, I asked about:

_____

During meditation, I saw how grateful I was for:

_____

During my meditation, I saw insight about:

_____

___ I visualized today.

While visualizing the things on my dream board,
I felt strongest about:

_____

While visualizing the things on my dream board,
I felt grateful for:

_____

While visualizing the things on my dream board,
I found I'm closer to reaching:

_____

___ I said my affirmations today.

I learned that I really can/do have:

_____

I realized that I am grateful for:

_____

I saw that I have grown in the area of:

_____

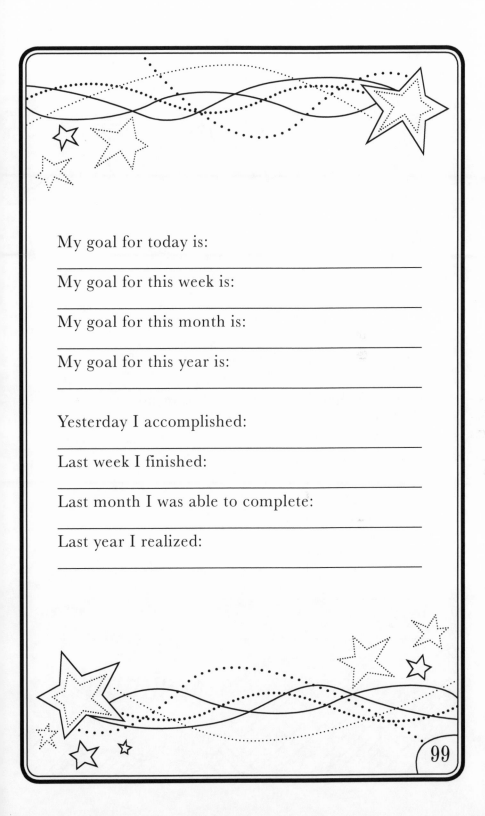

My goal for today is:

_____

My goal for this week is:

_____

My goal for this month is:

_____

My goal for this year is:

_____

Yesterday I accomplished:

_____

Last week I finished:

_____

Last month I was able to complete:

_____

Last year I realized:

_____

I've done all I can. The rest is up to you. I know you can do it because you've already made it this far. It's in your hands. Stay focused, determined and on track. If you get lost or distracted, forgive yourself and start again. Your effort is what will lead you to success. Keep at it and you will inevitably be living life for a living.

THE ~~end~~
Beginning
♡

Made in the USA
San Bernardino, CA
14 January 2014